Reading by Age 5

Using American Sign Language and Tucker Signing Strategies

Tucker, Bethanie H., Ed.D.
    Reading by Age 5: Using American Sign Language
    and Tucker Signing Strategies
Bethanie H. Tucker © 2007. 96 pp.
    ISBN-13: 978-1-929229-80-2
    ISBN-10: 1-929229-80-1

1. Reading   2. Education   3. Title

Also by Bethanie H. Tucker, Ed.D.

Tucker Signing Strategies for Reading

Mr. Base Ten Invents Mathematics

The Journey of Al & Gebra to the Land of Algebra

Reading by Age 5

Using American Sign Language and Tucker Signing Strategies

Bethanie H. Tucker, Ed.D.

Reading by Age 5 **involves the use of two sign languages:**

- American Sign Language

 and

- Tucker Signing Strategies for Reading

American Sign Language (ASL) signs represent ***words*** and ***concepts.***

Tucker Signs represent ***sounds.***

Both can contribute to a child's growth in language, decoding, and comprehension skills.

What the research says

1. Tucker Signing Strategies

Tucker Signing Strategies teach the sounds associated with letters and chunks of letters in a fast, fun way. Research has shown that students who learn the Tucker signs outperform their peers in word-recognition skills. Research reports can be found at www.ahaprocess.com.

2. American Sign Language

Research shows that learning a sign language, such as ASL, can:

- Improve children's early communications with their parents—whether the children are hearing-impaired or not.
- Help children to learn language more rapidly and more effectively than their peers.
- Enable infants to communicate their needs, therefore, showing fewer signs of frustration and crying less.
- Improve reading skills.
- Assist children in remembering words.
- Improve children's understanding of word meanings.
- Prompt children to pay closer attention by requiring them to watch the parent or teacher when signing or reading.

How does sign language help?

- When a child says and signs a word, he or she is remembering the word through auditory and kinesthetic means—through hearing *and* movement. Multi-modality strengthens recall and enhances oral-language development for reading comprehension.
- Tucker Signing Strategies support the development of phonemic awareness (the ability to hear, identify, and manipulate individual sounds in spoken words) and knowledge of printed letters and words (the understanding that letters make words).
- Children use their hands effortlessly and naturally.
- Knowing a second language boosts self-confidence.
- Babies can use signs to communicate.
- Eye contact deepens the bond between the child and the caregiver.
- The area of the brain that is used for language development shares nerve endings with the part of the brain responsible for motor coordination.
- Subject areas other than reading or spelling—including social studies, history, music, science, geography, and math—also can be enhanced with sign language.

The following books and research reports offer detailed information on each of these studies:

Allott, Robin. (1994). Gestural equivalents of language. Paper for Language Origins Society, University of California, Berkeley. Accessed June 26, 2006, at http://www.percepp.demon.co.uk/gesture.htm.

Daniels, Marilyn. (October 1994). The effects of sign language on hearing children's language development. *Communication Education.* 43.4: 291–298.

Daniels, Marilyn. (September 1996). Seeing language: the effect over time of sign language on vocabulary development in early childhood education. *Child Study Journal.* 26.3: 193–208.

Daniels, Marilyn. (2000). *Dancing with Words: Signing for Hearing Children's Literacy.* Westport, CT: Bergin & Garvey.

Felzer, Laura. (2000). Research on how signing helps hearing children learn to read. MBR Beginning Reading Program, California State Polytechnic University, Pomona. Accessed June 26, 2006, at http://www.csupomona.edu/~apfelzer/mbr/research.html.

Hafer, Jan C., & Wilson, Robert M. (1998). *Signing for Reading Success.* Washington, DC: Gallaudet University Press.

Moats, Louisa C. (1999). *Teaching Reading Is Rocket Science.* Washington, DC: American Federation of Teachers.

Nielsen, Diane C., & Luetke-Stahlman, Barbara. (Summer 2002). Phonological awareness: one key to the reading proficiency of deaf children. *American Annals of the Deaf.* 147.3: 11–17.

National Institute for Literacy. (2001). *Put Reading First.* Jessup, MD: ED Publications.

Roskos, Kathleen A., Christie, James F., & Richgels, Donald J. (March 2003). The essentials of early literacy instruction. *Young Children.* 52–60.

Wolfe, Patricia. (2001). *Brain Matters: Translating Research into Classroom Practice.* Alexandria, VA: Association for Supervision & Curriculum Development.

Table of Contents

Chapter 1
American Sign Language

Introduce the signs at a pace that is comfortable for your child or the children you teach. Depending on age and other developmental factors, some children can learn several phrases each day or week. Younger children should be taught the signs at a slower pace. Children as young as 9 months can learn to communicate through sign language.

Most children will need to see and to practice the signs several times before they can use them to communicate their needs and feelings.

> **Sign the words and phrases in Chapter 1 as often as possible throughout the day while talking to your child or students.**

Begin with the following sentence. Sign it over and over for several days or weeks until your child or students can sign each word effortlessly, then move on to the next word or sentence.

I love you.

 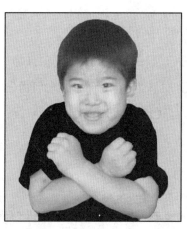 

I   love   you

Note: If your child is older than 1 or 2 years of age, try teaching several words or sentences each day.

I see you.

I   see   you

(Point two fingers toward your eyes, then
away from eyes, as if your fingertips are
looking at something in front of you.)

Remember: Look your child or students
in the eyes while signing.

baby

(Rock your arms as
if rocking a baby.)

---

happy

smile

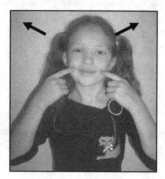

laugh

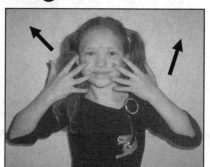

(Pat chest several times
with both hands, using
upward motion.)

Note: Show expression in your voice and on
your face when signing.

up

down

---

good

boy

(male)   (small)

(The sign for *male* looks like someone
taking off his cap.)

good

girl

(female)

(A girl ties her bonnet underneath her chin.)

(small)

Use these signs at every opportunity.

food, eat

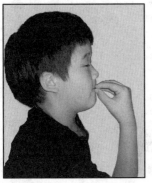

(Tap mouth several times with fingers.)

drink

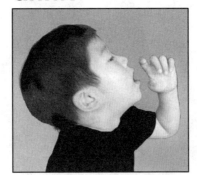

full

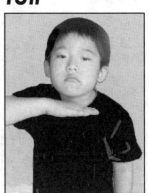

more

(Tap fingers together several times.)

please

(Rotate your hand in a circle on your chest.)

thank you

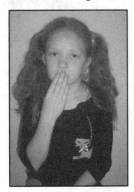

(Move your hand outward from your mouth as if throwing a kiss.)

Notes:

1. Many people sign *thank you* with two hands.
2. Many people sign *you're welcome* with the same sign as *thank you.*

nose

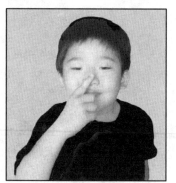

mouth

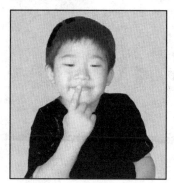

ear

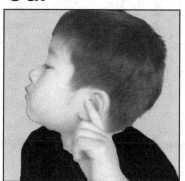

father

(male)

mother

(female)

Note: Some children will begin to use sign language at about 9 months.

brother

(male)   (same)

(Place two index
fingers together.)

sister

(female)   (same)

You are smart.
(It is not necessary to sign the word *are* in this sentence.)

you   *smart*

I will help you.

(It is not necessary to sign the word *will* in this sentence.)

I

help

(Move both hands
upward together.)

you

brush teeth

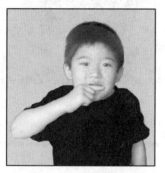

(Move finger as
if brushing teeth.)

drop

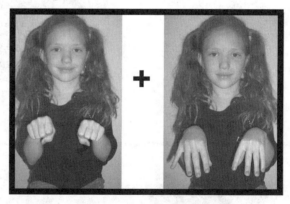

open   shut

I am proud of you.

(It is not necessary to sign the words *am* or *of* in this sentence.)

I

proud

(Move thumb upward
to show pride.)

you

Look at me.

(It is not necessary to sign the word *at* in this sentence.)

look

me

(Point two fingers toward your eyes, then away from
eyes, as if your fingertips are looking at something in
front of you.)

---

in  *out*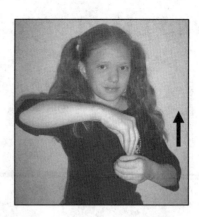

---

want

(Move hands
toward body.)

wait

(Wiggle fingers.)

time

(Point to "watch.")

---

stop

(Bring right hand downward
onto left hand.)

understand

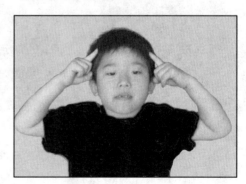

(Gently tap head.)

---

us

(Move hand from right to left.)

my

what

(Draw downward line on palm.)

name

now

(Drop hands
slightly downward.)

forget

know

(Tap forehead.)

don't know

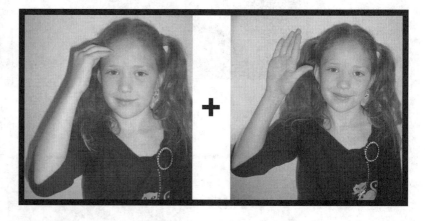

Tucker Signing Strategies

At about 3 years of age, children will be ready to look at letters, sign their sounds, and blend the sounds together to make words.

Tucker Signing Strategies signs can help children learn the sounds that letters represent in a fast, fun way.

The Tucker signs are different from ASL signs in two significant ways:

- Tucker signs are signed with the left hand. ASL signs are made with the right hand or with both hands.

- ASL signs are for talking to other people. Tucker signs are for talking to ourselves and for reading.

••

Have fun with your child or students while learning and using Tucker Signing Strategies!

Three Pointers for Teaching the Tucker Signs

1. Make each letter shape with your left hand. (Some letters look backward if you sign them with your right hand.) Also, signing with the left hand helps the brain to grow!

    Putting a glove on a child's left hand can help him/her to remember which hand to use for signing.

2. Some parents and teachers like to draw the letter on their hands with chalk or a washable marker. This makes the letter shape easier for their children to see.

3. Be sure to make the *letter sound* while holding or moving your hand as illustrated in each picture.

Have fun!

n

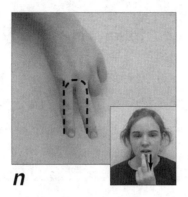

n

1. Show your child or students the letter *n* on your hand.
2. Put the letter *n* on your chin. Pull your chin down gently and make the *n* sound.
3. Help your child to sign the letter *n*. Be sure your child makes the *n* sound while signing the letter.

o

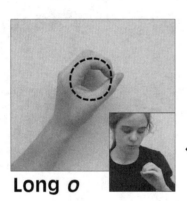

Long *o*

1. Show your child or students the letter *o* on your hand.
2. Stretch your arm out from your body (making your arm long) while making the long-*o* sound.
3. Help your child to sign the letter *o*. Be sure your child makes the long-*o* sound while signing the letter.

Sign the word *no*.

Make the *n* sign and then the *o* sign, blending the two sounds together to make the word *no*.

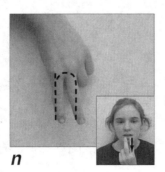

n

Long *o*

Question: How many signs should be taught in one day?

Answer: Teach the signs to your child or students at a pace that is comfortable for you and for them. Many children like to learn to read several words at one time. Others prefer to move more slowly.

g

1. Ball the fingers of your left hand into a fist.
2. Show your child the letter g on your left hand as pictured.
3. Tap your left hand to your throat while making the g sound.

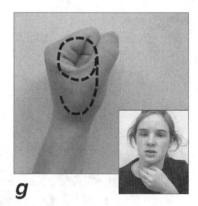

g

Sign the word go.

Make the g sign and then the o sign, blending the two sounds together to make the word go.

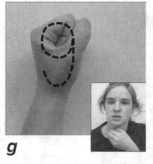

g

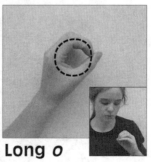

Long o

m

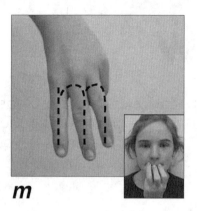

1. Show your child or students the *m* shape on your left hand.
2. Put your fingertips to your lips and make the *m* sound.

m

---

e

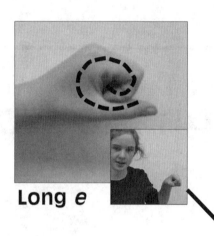

1. Show your child or students the *e* shape on your left hand.
2. Stretch your arm out from your body (making your arm long). Make the *e* sound while stretching your arm.

Long *e*

Sign the word *me*.

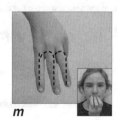

m

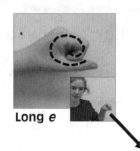

Long *e*

W

1. Show your child or students the w shape on your left hand.
2. Put your fingertips to your throat and make the w sound.

w

Sign the word we.

w

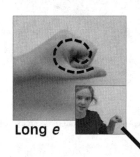

Long *e*

Try to find each new word in a newspaper or magazine. Sign the word each time you find it.

The letter *y* represents more than one sound. This lesson teaches one of the sounds that *y* represents.

y

1. Form a y shape with your left hand.
2. Point to your eye with your y-shaped left hand.
3. Stretch your arm out from your body (making your arm long).
4. Make the i sound while moving your arm.

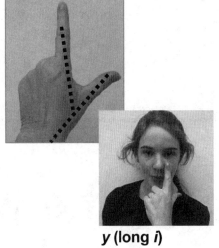

y (long *i*)

Sign the word *my*.

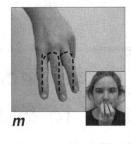

m

y (long *i*)

h

1. Show your child or students the *h* shape on your left hand.
2. Put your *h*-shaped hand in front of your mouth and make the *h* sound.

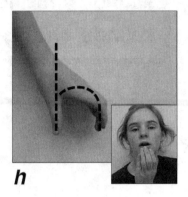

h

Sign the word *he*.

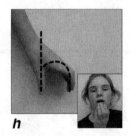

h

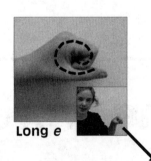

Long *e*

Hint: Ask your child to write each word that he or she learns to read.

www.ahaprocess.com

S

1. With your left hand, draw the letter s in the air.
2. Make the s sound while drawing the s shape.

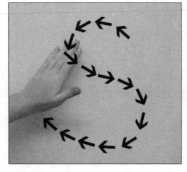

s

Sign the word see.

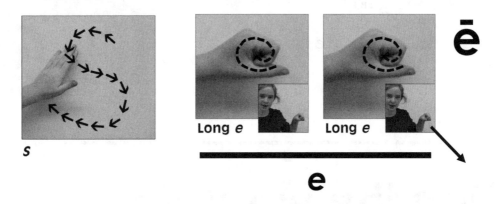

s

Long *e*   Long *e*

ē

e

(Sign the e sound only once.)

Explain to your child that *ee* in the word *see* makes one *e* sound because the two letters work together. Therefore, we sign the *e* sound only once in this word.

U

1. Show your child or students the *u* shape on your left hand.
2. Tap your chin with your *u*-shaped hand while making the short-*u* sound.

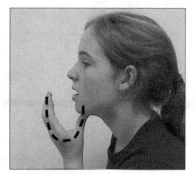

Short *u*

---

p

1. Show your child or students the *p* shape on your left hand.
2. Put your *p*-shaped hand in front of your mouth and make the *p* sound.

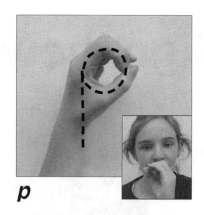

p

Sign the word *up*.

Short *u*

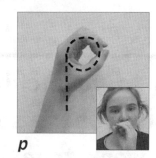

p

c

1. Show your child or students the c shape on your left hand.
2. Move your fingers in a cutting motion. Make the hard-c sound (sounds like a *k*) while "cutting" with your fingers.

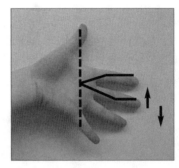

c

Sign the word *cup.*

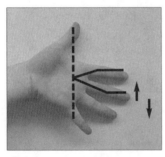

c

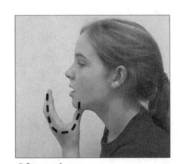

Short *u*

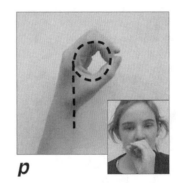

p

Just for fun, sign the words *pun* and *sun.*

r

1. Move your left hand upward in an *r* shape.
2. Make the *r* sound while moving your hand.

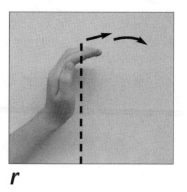

r

Sign the word *run*.

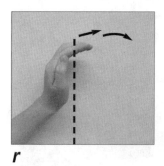

r

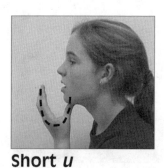

Short *u*

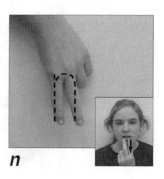

n

Just for fun, sign the word *rug*.

f

1. Show your child or students the *f* shape on your left hand.
2. Put your *f*-shaped hand in front of your mouth and make the *f* sound.

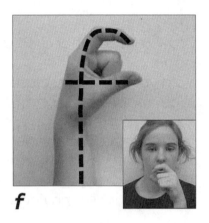

f

Sign the word *fun*.

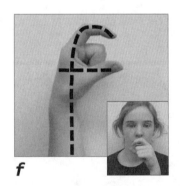

f

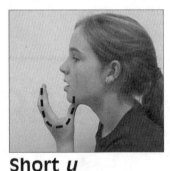

Short *u*

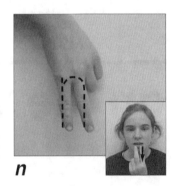

n

Just for fun, sign the word *free*.

Short a

1. Draw a large letter *a* on a sheet of paper.
2. Hold your left hand close to your face, making your arm "short."
3. Rotate your left arm in a circle as if tracing the round shape of the letter *a* with your left arm.
4. Make the short-*a* sound (as in the word *cat*) while moving your arm.

Short *a*

---

t

1. Draw a straight vertical line on a sheet of paper.
2. Pretend the line is the vertical part of the letter *t*.
3. Pretend to cross the letter *t* with your left hand as pictured.
4. Make the *t* sound while crossing the letter *t* in the air.

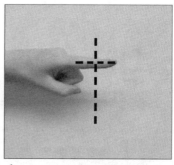

t

Sign the word cat.

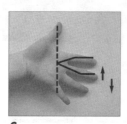

c

Short *a*

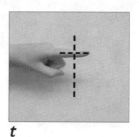

t

Just for fun, sign the words *tag, can, man, pan, tan, hat, mat, pat, rat,* and *sat.*

www.ahaprocess.com

b

1. Draw the letter *b* on a sheet of paper.
2. Point out that the straight line comes before the circle in the letter *b*.
3. Make a straight line with your left hand.
4. Pretend that your left hand is a bat. Let your left hand strike an imaginary ball several times.
5. Make the *b* sound while making the *b* sign.

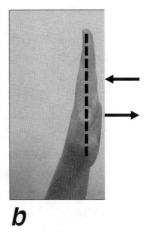

b

Sign the word *bat*.

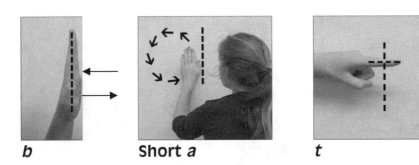

b   Short *a*   *t*

> Just for fun, sign the words *bun, hub, bus, bag,* and *bug*.

d

1. Draw a large letter *d* on a sheet of paper.
2. Point out that the circle comes before the straight line in the letter *d*; therefore, the sign for the letter *d* is a circle.
3. Make a circle shape with your left hand.
4. Wiggle your left hand and make the *d* sound, pretending that the circle is a dog's nose, and the dog is digging, making the *d* sound.

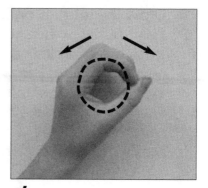

d

Sign the word *dad.*

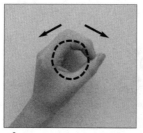

d

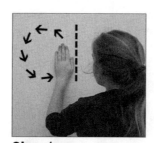

Short *a*

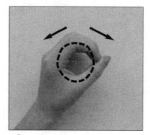

d

> ### Just for fun, sign the words *deep, drag, bad,* and *pad.*

Short *i*

1. Point to your eye with your left hand.
2. Make your arm "short" while making the short-*i* sign (as in the word *it*).
3. Make the short-*i* sound while pointing to your eye.

Short *i*

Sign the word *dig.*

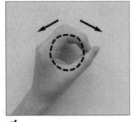

d

Short *i*

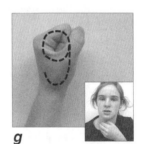

g

Just for fun, sign the words *big, fig, pig, rig, wig, din, fin, pin, nip, rip, sip,* and *tip.*

L

1. Pretend to draw an *L* shape in the air with your left hand.
2. Make the *L* sound while drawing the *L* shape in the air.

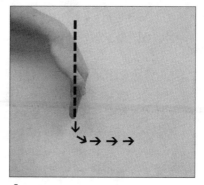

L

Sign the word *lip*.

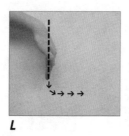

L

Short *i*

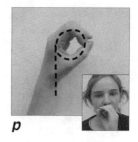

p

Just for fun, sign the words
lid, flip, and *slip*.

j

1. Pretend to draw the *j* shape in the air with your left hand.
2. Make the *j* sound while drawing the *j* shape.

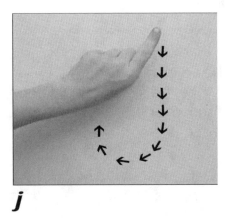

j

Sign the word je͟ep.
e

j

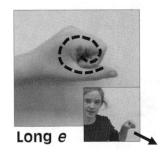

Long *e*

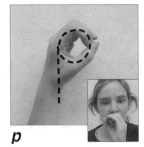

p

Just for fun, sign the words
jig, jump, and *jam.*

X

1. Make an x shape with your left hand as pictured.
2. Make the x sound while forming the x shape.

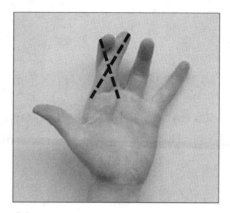

x

Sign the word *six*.

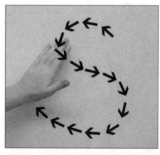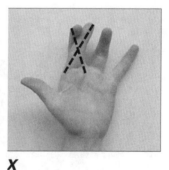

s   **Short *i***   *x*

Just for fun, sign the words *next, text, ox, box, fox,* and *pox.*

z

1. Draw a z shape in the air as pictured.
2. Make the z sound while drawing the z shape.

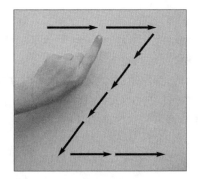

z

Sign the word *zip*.

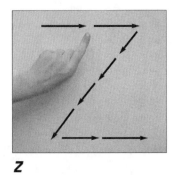

z

Short *i*

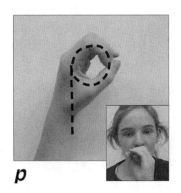

p

> Just for fun, sign the words
> *zest*, *buzz*, and *fuzz*.

k

1. Draw a k shape on your left hand as pictured.
2. Move your second and third fingers in a cutting motion.
3. Make the k sound while "cutting" with your fingers.

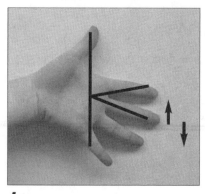

k

Sign the word *kit*.

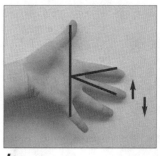

k

Short *i*

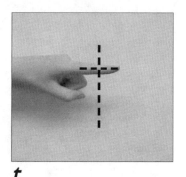

t

Just for fun, sign the word *kitten*.

---

www.ahaprocess.com

V

1. Make a v shape on your left hand.
2. Place your v-shaped hand on your throat.
3. Make the v sound and feel the vibrations in your throat while making the v sound.

v

Sign the word *van.*

v

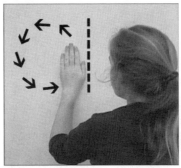

Short *a*

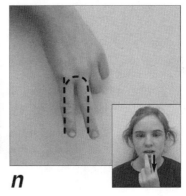

n

Just for fun, sign the words
vat and *vast.*

This chapter will help you to teach your child or students about letter 'buddies'—letters that get together and make a new sound.

Examples of letter buddies are:

sh	*ou*
ir	*ow*
er	*ch*
ur	*ar*
au	*qu*
aw	*tion*
th	*ing*
wh	

sh

Put the index finger of your left hand to your lips while making the *sh* sound.

sh

ir

Make an upward spiraling motion in the air with your left hand while making the *ir* sound.

er/ir/ur

er/ir/ur

Note: The signs for the buddies *er*, *ir*, and *ur* are all the same!

Sign the word *shirt*.

sh

er/ir/ur

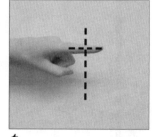

t

Just for fun, sign the words *ship*, *shift*, *bird*, *turn*, *fern*, *perm*, *hurl*, *sir*, and *girl*.

OW

1. Show your child or students the letters o and w on your left hand as pictured.
2. Shake your hand while making the ow sound (as in the word cow).

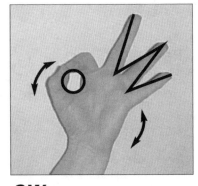

ow

Sign the word *shower.*

sh   *ow*   *er/ir/ur*

Just for fun, sign the words *cow, how, now, wow, plow, down, gown, town, clown, cower, power, tower,* and *flower.*

OU

1. Review the ow sign.
2. Explain to your child or students that the *ou* sign is the same as the ow sign.

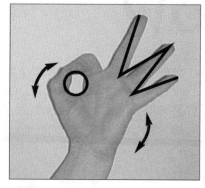

ou

Sign the word *shout*.

 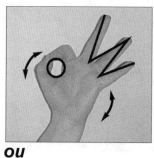 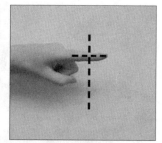

sh   *ou*   *t*

> Just for fun, sign the words *gout, pout, count, mount, noun, found, hound, round, sound, ground, loud, cloud, bound,* and *pound.*

ch

1. Make a c shape with your left hand as pictured.
2. Move your hand forward like a train moving down a track.
3. Make the ch sound while moving your hand.

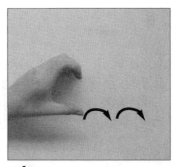

ch

Sign the word church.

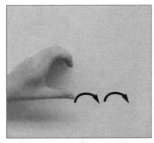

ch

er/ir/ur

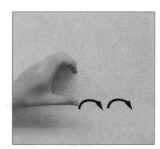

ch

Just for fun, sign the words *cheek, cheep, chat, chow, chirp, churn, bunch, lunch, punch, crunch, much, such, chap,* and *chunk.*

ar

1. Move your hand forward in the air (like a lion pawing at someone).
2. Make the *ar* sound (as in the word *dark*) while moving your arm.

ar

Sign the word *shark*.

sh

ar

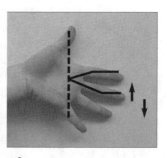

k

Just for fun, sign the words *bark, dark, hark, lark, mark, park, tart, bar, car, far, jar, carp, sharp, cart, dart, mart, part, chart, barn, farm, harm, farmer,* and *charm.*

th

th

1. Stick your tongue out and pretend to touch your tongue with the index finger of your left hand.
2. Make the *th* sound (as in the word *thump*) while pretending to touch your tongue.

Sign the word *thump*.

  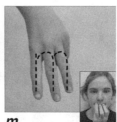 

th   Short *u*   *m*   *p*

Just for fun, sign the words *thin, that, bath, path,* and *lather.*

---

wh

1. Show your child or students the w shape on your left hand as pictured.
2. Brush your left hand downward across your face while making the *wh* sound.

wh

Sign the word why.

wh

y (long i)

> ## Just for fun, sign the words *whip* and *whirl.*

aw

1. Hold your left hand beside your face.
2. Drop your hand forward while making the *aw* sound (as in the word *saw*).

aw

Sign the word *saw*.

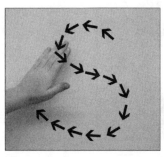

s

aw

Just for fun, sign the words *jaw, law, paw, raw, thaw, crawl,* and *shawl.*

Note: The sign for **au** is the same as the sign for **aw**!

au

Sign the word *haul*.

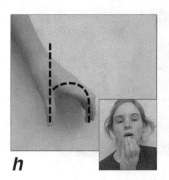

h

au

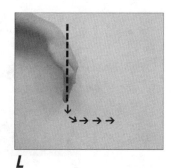

L

Just for fun, sign the words *maul* and *Paul.*

all

The sign for *all* is the *au* and *L* signs blended together.

1. Make the *au* sign, then immediately make the *L* sign.
2. Make the *all* sound while moving your hand.

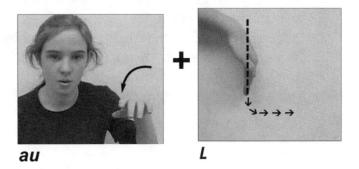

au + *L*

Sign the word call.

c *au* + *L*

> ## Just for fun, sign the words *ball, fall, mall, tall,* and *wall.*

qu

1. Show your child or students the *u* shape on your left hand. Explain that in the English language the letter *q* is almost always followed by the letter *u*.
2. Explain that the word *queen* begins with *qu*.
3. Circle your face with your *u*-shaped left hand, as if your face is the queen's face.
4. Make the *qu* sound (sounds like *kw*) while moving your hand.

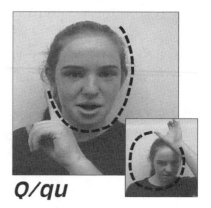

Q/qu

Sign the word quit.

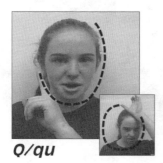  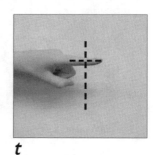

Q/qu   Short *i*   *t*

Just for fun, sign the words
quill and *quip*.

tion

1. Hold your left hand in front of your face like you're preparing to make the *t* sign.
2. As if suddenly noticing that this letter *t* is with his buddies *i, o,* and *n,* and therefore makes a different sound, move your hand from the side of your face into the *sh* sign.
3. Make the *tion* sound (as in the word *motion*) while moving your hand.

tion

Sign the word caption.

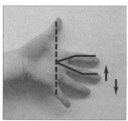

c

Short *a*

p

tion

> **Just for fun, sign the words *lotion, motion, emotion,* and *devotion.***

ing

1. Make the short-*i* sign, then make the *n* sign, and then the *g* sign.
2. Blend the three signs together into one rapid, smooth movement.

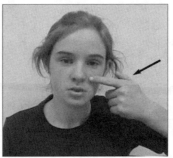

ing

Short *i*

n

g

Sign the word *sing*.

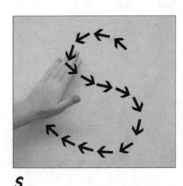

s

ing

> **Just for fun, sign the words**
> *ping, ring, wing, bring, cling,*
> *fling, thing,* **and** *linger.*

Explain to your child or students that the English language is very exciting because the letters

a, e, i, o, u, and *y*

can stand for more than one sound!

We call these letters *vowels*.

Sometimes the vowels are brave and say their names; we call them long vowels.

Sometimes the vowels sound shy; we call them short vowels.

Chapter 4 explains the sounds that long and short vowels can represent.

A, E, I, O, U, and Y are vowels.

Each vowel makes two or more sounds—a long-vowel sound and a short-vowel sound.

We have already learned one sound for each vowel. In this chapter we will learn a second sound for each one.

Sing the following song to the tune of "The Alphabet Song."

Verse 1

A, e, i, o, u, and y ...
Vowels are fun, I'll tell you why;
There's a vowel in every word, *
Every word you've ever heard;
A, e, i, o, u, and y ...
Vowels are fun, now you know why!

Verse 2

A, e, i, o, u, and y ...
Vowels are fun, I'll tell you why;
Some vowels are short, and some are long,
Short vowels sound shy, long vowels sound strong;
A, e, i, o, u, and y ...
Vowels are fun, now you know why!

* with at least one notable exception: *nth*, as in *nth* degree

Short e

The letter *e* makes more than one sound: long *e*, as in the word *me*, and short *e*, as in the word *met*. We have already learned the long-e sign (as in *me*). Now we will learn the sign for short *e*.

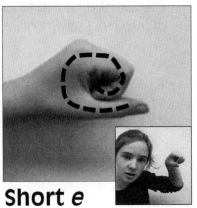

Short *e*

1. Show your child or students the *e* shape on your left hand.
2. Hold your left hand close to your face (with a short arm). Make the short-e sound while holding your left hand beside your face.

Sign the word *met*.

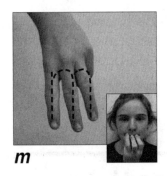

m

Short *e*

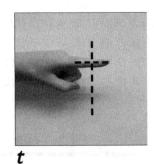

t

> Just for fun, sign the words *bet, let, net, pet, set, Ben, den, hen, men, pen, ten, fell, sell, tell, chess, best, nest, pest, rest, test, west,* and *question.*

Silent e

Sometimes the letter e is long, and sometimes it is short, but the letter e also has another job. Sometimes it is silent!

The silent e at the end of a word helps the other vowel in the word to be brave and say its name (it makes the other vowel long).

1. Make the e shape with your left hand.
2. Cover the e shape with your right hand.

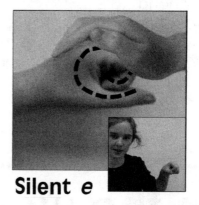

Silent _e_

The letter e in the word _rake_ is silent. It helps the _a_ to be brave (long).
The letter e in the word _smile_ is silent. It helps the _i_ to be brave (long).
The letter e in the word _bone_ is silent. It helps the _o_ to be brave (long).
The letter e in the word _mule_ is silent. It helps the _u_ to be brave (long).

Just for fun, sign the words _joke, choke, code, mole, pole, role, bone, cone, lone, tone, dome, home, cope, hope, mope, rope, dose, close, dote, mote, note, vote, stroke,_ and _crane._

Long *i*

The letter *i* makes two sounds: short *i*, as in the word *lip*, and long *i*, as in the word *line*. We have already learned the short-*i* sign (as in *lip*). Now we will learn the sign for long *i*.

1. Point to your eye.
2. Stretch your arm out (making your arm long).
3. Make the long-*i* sound while moving your arm.

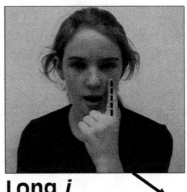

Long *i*

Sign the word *like*.

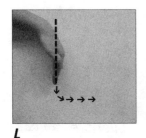
L

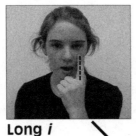
Long *i*

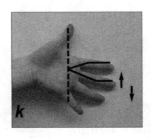
k

Silent *e*

Just for fun, sign the words *life, wife, bike, hike, like, mike, hide, tide, wide, chide, dine, fine, line, mine, nine, pine, twine, dime, lime, mime, time,* and *crime.*

Long a

The letter *a* makes two sounds: short *a*, as in the word *rat*, and long *a*, as in the word *make*. We have already learned the short-*a* sign (as in *rat*). Now we'll learn the long-*a* sign.

1. Stretch your arm out nice and long.
2. Rotate your left arm in a circle, as if tracing the circular shape of the letter *a*.
3. Make the *a* sound while moving your hand.

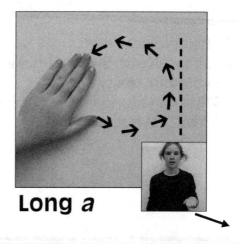

Long *a*

Sign the word *make*.

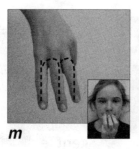 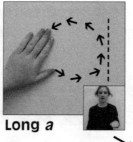 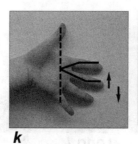 

m Long *a* *k* Silent *e*

Just for fun, sign the words *bake, cake, fake, lake, make, rake, sake, take, cave, gave, pave, rave, save,* and *wave*.

Short o

The letter o makes two sounds: long o, as in the word *no,* and short o, as in the word *pot.* We have already learned the long-o sign (as in the word *no*). Now we will learn the short-o sign.

1. Show your child or students the o shape on your left hand.
2. Hold the o sign close to your face (making your arm short).
3. Make the short-o sound.

Short *o*

Sign the word *pot.*

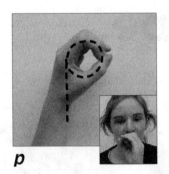

p

Short *o*

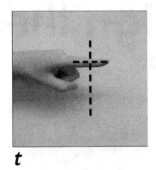

t

Just for fun, sign the words *cot, dot, got, hot, jot, lot, not, rot, tot, blot, dog, fog, hog, log, clog, hop, mop, sop, clop, flop, glop, cob, rob, sob, god, nod, pod, rod, mom, Tom,* and *Don.*

Long *u*

The letter *u* makes two sounds: short *u*, as in the word *cup*, and long *u*, as in the word *tube*. We have already learned the short-*u* sign (as in *cup*). Now we will learn the long-*u* sign.

1. Show your child or students the *u* shape on your left hand.
2. Stretch your arm out nice and long, as if pointing to someone.
3. Make the long-*u* sound as you move your arm.

Long *u*

Sign the word *tube*.

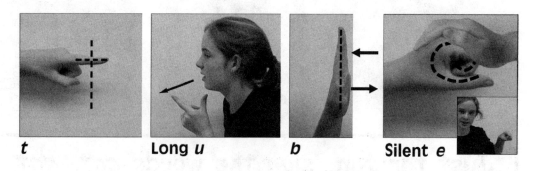

| *t* | Long *u* | *b* | Silent *e* |

> ## Just for fun, sign the words *cute* and *chute*.

www.ahaprocess.com

Long y

The letter y makes two vowel sounds: Y at the end of a short word sounds like i, as in the words *my, by, try,* and *shy.* Y at the end of a long (two-syllable) word sounds like e, as in *funny, sunny,* and *penny.* We have already learned the sign for short y (y that sounds like i). Now we will learn the sign for long y (y that sounds like e).

1. Hold your left hand in the air, shaped like the letter y.
2. Bring your fingers down into the shape of the e sign.
3. Make the e sound while moving your fingers.

y (long e)

Sign the word *bumpy.*

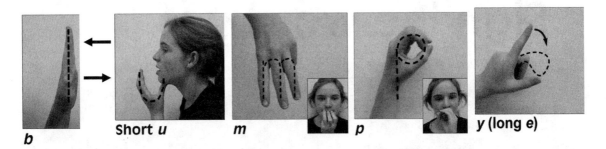

b   Short *u*   *m*   *p*   *y* (long e)

> **Just for fun, sign the words** *bunny, funny, runny, sunny, dummy, gummy, tummy, buggy, muggy, buddy, muddy, ruddy, nippy, nutty, witty, dirty, flirty, jerky,* **and** *perky.*

Consonant y

The letter y is *really* special.

We have already learned that the letter y makes two vowel sounds, as in the words *my* and *penny*. Now we will learn that the letter y also can be a consonant, as in the word *yes*.

1. Show your child or students the letter y on your left hand.
2. Point your index finger (the point of the letter y) into your mouth.
3. Make the y sound, as in the word *yes*, while pointing.

y (consonant)

Sign the word yes.

   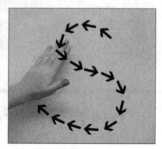

y (consonant)   **Short *e***   ***s***

> ## Just for fun, sign the words *yam*, *yet*, and *yoyo*.

Soft *g*

Sometimes the letter *g* makes the *j* sound, as in the word *gem*. We call this the soft-*g* sound.

1. Make the *g* shape with your left hand.
2. Move your hand, as if drawing the letter *j* in the air.
3. Make the *j* sound as you move your hand.

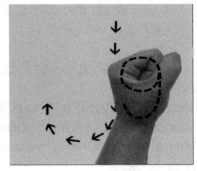

g

Sign the word *gem*.

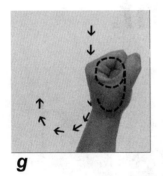  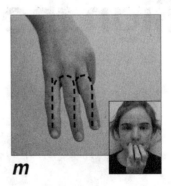

g   Short *e*   *m*

> ## Just for fun, sign the word *gentle*.
> ## (The *tle* ending can be signed *t*, *l*, silent *e*.)

Soft c

Sometimes the letter c makes the k sound, as in the word cat. We call this the hard-c sound. Sometimes the letter c makes the s sound, as in the word cent. We call this the soft-c sound. We have already learned the hard-c sign. Now we will learn the soft-c sign.

1. Make the c shape with your left hand.
2. Move your hand forward, like a pair of scissors tearing something.
3. Make the s sound as you move your hand.

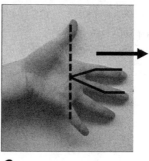

c

Hint: The c is usually soft when it is followed by an e, i, or y.

Sign the word cent.

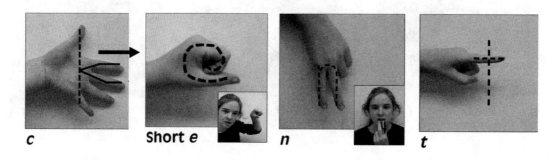

c   Short e   n   t

Just for fun, sign the words city, circle, circus, and cite.

---

ck

In words such as *sock* and *rack*, the letters *c* and *k* make the same sound. Therefore, when signing the *ck* combination in words such as these, simply sign either the *c* or the *k*. It is not necessary to sign both letters.

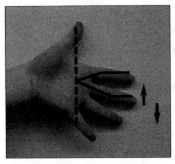

c

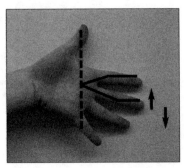

k

Just for fun, sign the words *back, Jack, lack, Mack, pack, rack, sack, tack, crack, whack, deck, neck, Becky, fleck, lick, nick, pick, Rick, sick, tick, flick, slick, dock, hock, jock, lock, mock, rock, sock, block, clock, flock, pocket, buck, duck, luck, muck,* **and** *cluck.*

That Silly Letter s

Sometimes the letter s sounds like a z, as in the word *business*.

You can sign the z when looking at the letter s in the following words:

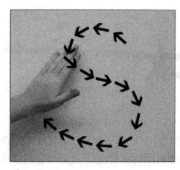

s

busy, *is, his, misery, hose, nose, pose, rose, chose,* and *close*

bu_siness
z

Some words have tricky parts!

The *ph* in the word *phone* sounds like an *f*.

phone
___
f

When you sign this word, make the *f* sign when you look at the *ph*.

> Just for fun, sign the words *graph*, *phase*, *Phil*, *Phillip*, *phobic*, *phonetic*, *phonics*, *phony*, *photograph*, and *sphinx*.

Some words have silent letters!

The *gh* combination in the word *naughty* is silent.

nau*gh*ty

When signing this word, cross your arms across your chest when you look at the *gh*, then make no sound.

Just for fun, sign the words *fight, might, night, right, sight, tight, flight, fright,* and *caught.*

Vowel Teams

Sometimes vowels work in teams. For example, in the word *team*, the e and a are a team. Together they make the long-e sound.

t<u>ea</u>m
e

Some people say, "When two vowels go walking, the first one does the talking." Others simply say two vowels side by side make the sound of the first vowel.

Other words that have vowel teams are:

lain	*beam*	*boat*
main	*seam*	*coat*
pain	*team*	*goat*
rain	*cream*	*moat*
brain	*dream*	*float*
Spain	*gleam*	*soap*
twain	*mean*	

In each of the above words the first vowel says its name, while the second vowel is silent.

Sight Words

Some words do not follow the rules; therefore, we do not sign them. We must simply learn to recognize them upon sight. We call them "sight words."

The following sight words do not follow the rules. Maybe we should send them to "time-out" for breaking the rules!

Time out!

ancient	one
antique	read
both	should
bread	the
break	their
buy	there
come	thought
could	to
do	two
does	want
dove	was
eye	were
future	what
give	where
has	who
have	woman
is	won
love	world
none	would
of	you
old	young

Now It's Your Turn to Be Creative!

You and your child or students can have fun making up your own signs for:

- *oo as in boo, too, cool, tool, drool*

- *oo as in book, cook, hook, look, nook, rook, took, crook, shook*

- *oi as in oil, boil, foil, soil, toil*

- *oy as in boy, coy, toy*

- *or as in for, nor, more, shore*

… and any other signs that you want to make up!

There's no "right" or "wrong" way to sign these sounds.

Be as creative as you would like!

Looking at Literature

Find stories you can read and sign to your child or students, such as the following. You can sign with ASL, or you can sign some of the sounds or words with the Tucker signs.

hop

Hop.

Hop.

Hop.

Stop.

Try signing this modified version of "Mary Had a Little Lamb."

Make the _L_ sign whenever you read the letter _L_ in the following poem.

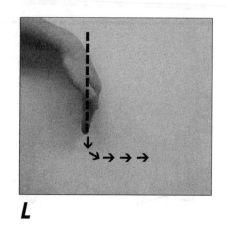

_L_

Lucy had a little lamb,
Little lamb,
Little lamb ...

Lucy had a little lamb,
Its legs were long and low.

'Peter, Peter, Pumpkin Eater'

1. Read the nursery rhyme out loud to your child or students.
2. Reread the nursery rhyme. Make the *er/ir/ur* sign while reading the underlined parts of the words.

er/ir/ur

Pet<u>er</u>, Pet<u>er</u>, pumpkin eat<u>er</u>,
Had a wife but couldn't keep h<u>er</u>.

Now he's neat<u>er</u>,
Now he's sweet<u>er</u>.
Maybe now Pet<u>er</u>
Can keep h<u>er</u>.

agree

(think + same)

anger

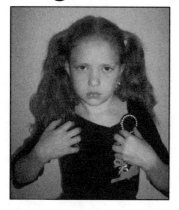

busy

cry

don't want

friend

hope

next

(Move right hand from behind to in front of left hand.)

obey

sad

stand

this

understand

walk

which

who

(Circle mouth with finger.)

Don't stop!

Add any other positive signs that you would like. Many bookstores carry excellent books on ASL.

Also, keep practicing the Tucker signs. And remember, have fun!

<u>NOTES</u>

NOTES

Process, Inc.

www.ahaprocess.com

aha! Process, Inc.
P.O. Box 727, Highlands, TX 77562
(800) 424-9484; fax: (281) 426-5600;
store@ahaprocess.com

ORDER FORM

Please send me:

_____ COPY/COPIES of *Reading by Age 5* book (with DVD)

BOOKS: $39.00/each + $4.50 first book, + $2.00 each additional book, shipping/handling

UPS SHIP-TO ADDRESS (no post office boxes, please):

NAME _____

ORGANIZATION _____

ADDRESS _____

_____

PHONE(S) _____

E-MAIL ADDRESS(ES) _____

_____

METHOD OF PAYMENT:

PURCHASE ORDER # _____
PLEASE NOTE: Signed copy of purchase order must be submitted with completed order form.

CREDIT CARD TYPE _____ EXP _____

CREDIT CARD # _____

CHECK $ _____ CHECK # _____

SUBTOTAL $ _____

SHIPPING $ _____

SALES TAX $ _____ 6.25% IN TEXAS

TOTAL $ _____

More eye-openers at ...

www.ahaprocess.com

- **Join our aha! Process News List!**

  - Receive the latest income and poverty statistics *free* when you join!
  - Also receive a free downloadable copy of ***Understanding Learning***!
  - Then receive periodic news and updates, recent articles written by Dr. Ruby K. Payne, and much more!

- **Subscribe to *Signs They Are Learning*, an e-newsletter**

  - Receive ideas for additional mental models in all disciplines

- **Visit our online store for other related titles**
  - *Mr. Base Ten Invents Mathematics* by Dr. Bethanie H. Tucker
  - *The Journey of Al & Gebra to the Land of Algebra* by Dr. Tucker
  - *Tucker Take-Home Books* by Melinda C. Ausband (accompanying student materials for *Tucker Signing Strategies*)

- **Register for Dr. Payne's U.S. National Tour on *A Framework for Understanding Poverty***

- **Learn about our Trainer Certification Programs**